GREAT MOMS OF THE BIBLE

A GUIDE FOR CHRISTIAN MOTHERS TODAY

GUERLINE REID

HARVESTERS ONLINE LLC

CONTENTS

I

INTRODUCTION

A satanic system is operating in the world today to break down motherhood. The serpent—the cunning beast from the Garden of Eden—has devised a system to alienate mothers from their children.

With a world that is losing its moral compass, calling evil good and good evil, a mother's place in their children's lives becomes a greater guidepost for living. Good mothers have to stand up and say enough is enough; we will take the authority that God has given us and speak to our children. God calls for us to speak His word as the guiding light for our children, and not be silent.

Mothers of faith have to stand up against all the odds and train their children in Biblical beliefs and morality. She is the guard at the door, blocking access to her children's vulnerabilities and weaknesses.

The serpent knows that if she is at the door, her children can grow strong and crush his works in society. So, a mom's actions and behavior must be intentional, wielding them as weapons against Satan's beastly system, and as tools for building her children's character.

Mothers are visionaries. No matter where she is culturally, environmentally, or nationally, her children are always the center of why she is called a mother. She never limits the vision of her children to what they are in the present, but she meets them in the future by nurturing, protecting, and praying that God will keep them from the hands of evil.

In times past, the great mothers would wear one dress and save money so that their children could go to school. She would go hungry so that she could feed her young. She stops at nothing so her children can survive. A great mom lays down her very life so her children can excel.

In today's modern society, the term mother is redefined as the role of women is challenged by the confusing idea that any gender can give birth. However, the testimonies of women from Bible times to the present show who are the great mothers. The great mothers endure, pray, build, and sometimes fight to elevate the lives of their children.

2

GREAT MOMS STRENGTHEN THEIR CHILDREN'S IDENTITY

EVE

And Adam knew his wife again; and she bare a
son, and called his name Seth: For God, said she,
hath appointed me another seed instead of Abel,
whom Cain slew.

Genesis 4:25

E ve was the first mother in the Bible. She understood that
her children had an appointment from God. Her job
was to make sure that the appointment came to pass and that
her children were consecrated unto the Lord.

She Understood that Her Son Was Appointed by God

She spoke with faith and boldness, believing that her child would receive what seemed to have been lost. God told her that there would be a war between her seed and the devil's seed (Genesis 3:15). Good mothers understand that there is a separation between good *and evil*. She understands there is a spiritual separation between her seed and the devil's seed.

Her Mothering Continued Despite Disappointments

Eve must have been disappointed when her first son, Cain, killed her second son, Abel. The loss must have been hurtful. Sometimes, as mothers, our disappointments can attach themselves to our children, and they can feel obligated to carry unnecessary weight.

But good moms don't allow disappointments to obstruct their role in raising children who accomplish God's appointment. Great mothers teach their children that disappointment is just a way for the appointment to be established.

I can imagine Eve reminding God that she needs an appointed seed to fight against the attacks of the serpent—the devil—against her and mankind. She never blamed anyone for what took place in her household, but she kept her eyes on God's promise. A good mom learns that she plays a primary role in making sure that her children fulfill their destiny. Moms understand that a child needs a godly environment to nurture their destiny.

She Nurtured Her Children in God's Promise

Although today's mothering is not an easy task, moms have to make sure that their children are following the path of the word of God. Children need guidance, protection, and a way of escape, and mothers have the intuition to make sure that their children understand who they are and what they represent. Eve acknowledged that her seed was appointed and that God was the one who gave her child. We, as mothers, cannot treat our children any way that we want because God is the one who appoints them.

How mothers see their children will determine how they see themselves. The Bible says, "Before I formed thee in the belly I knew thee..." (Jeremiah 1:5). God knows who our children are. Children are not given without a purpose; it is up to moms to nourish that purpose with the word of God.

What We Learn from Eve's Example

- Acknowledge God's purpose for your child.

- Believe in God for your child even in the face of disappointment.

- Raise your child in the hope that God's promise for him will come to pass.

LEAH

And she conceived again, and bare a son: and she said, Now will I praise the LORD: therefore she called his name Judah; and left bearing.

Genesis 29:35

Although in today's society, we name our children randomly based on our wishes or feelings, in bible times names had meaning and attachment. Leah was going through afflictions, loneliness, and resentment.

Her husband, Jacob, was not fond of her. He intended to marry Leah's younger sister, Rachel, but he was tricked into marrying Leah first. Jacob married Leah's sister after agreeing with her father to work for him for an additional seven years.

So, Leah was the unloved one of Jacob's two wives. However, she had a job to do when she became a mother. She would not allow her personal feelings or her emotions to get in the way of raising her children.

She gave them names that would open heaven's door and engulf the ears of her God. The more she named her children, the more God blessed her. When life is a reproach, as a mom, you can turn it around with your children and by being a good mom.

She Named Her Children for Victory

Leah was hated, and she was afflicted, but she understood the power of naming her children. Every time a trial came her way, she reacted by naming and identifying her children.

The meaning of the name Reuben, her first son, was *'Behold, a son'*. Leah realized that God saw her situation and delivered her by giving her a son. Her son represented deliverance from her adverse situation.

Leah would not allow her children to go through an identity crisis. She used her situation to testify of God's favor on her and her children. Leah recognized that life circumstances do not mean that God is not watching, nor does it mean her children would be nameless.

She conquered the thought that her children would be outcasts, fatherless, or a proverb. She instilled character, resilience, and growth in her children.

Simeon, her second-born son's name, meant *'God hears'*. She was testifying that God had heard her cries in her troubles. The third son was Levi, meaning *'Joined'*, because Leah believed that now her husband would draw closer to her, or be joined to her. So, her third son represented a closer bond between her and her husband.

For Leah, her children represented her victory over her circumstances. She gave an identity of victory to her children, rather than one that was based on her own problems. Therefore, her third son Judah's name meant *'Praise'*.

Good moms call their children names that root them in an identity of victory. This is not simply speaking of their given names, but what we call and say about our children.

The world's system will not shake their mind or their spirit because they know and understand the value of their name. Great moms teach their children that they are not to identify themselves with the circumstances of the world but with God's work of grace.

As a mother, even if you are going through trials, you can still teach your children to live by the identity that Christ has given them. By doing so, they will learn to love their identity in Christ. It is a beautiful thing when a child sees a mother treat them like royalty, even in peasantry circumstances. The child will understand the power their name represents. And the world will not just see a face, but a person imbued with divine purpose.

Each name of Leah's children was a reminder that she overcame hatred and adversity. Through her declaration, they became a showcase of victory, answered prayers, household stability, and praise to God. Leah found whatever was of a good report and made that the representation for her children.

Build Your Child's Identity in God

The rise of digital and social media makes it hard for children to live with a godly identity. Children are bombarded with ideas from the online world that conflict with God's word.

Many young people adopt an alien identity through social media, separate from the ones they learned from their parents, from a plethora of gender identities to non-biblical causes.

There is a fight in the spirit realm that mothers have to come against so that the identity of their children according to Biblical principles, remains in place. Therefore, it is important to call children by what God has for them.

Leah's first four sons were like an army given to revive God's favor upon her life. To call your children by a name that can outlive the present circumstances requires prophetic insight, seeing beyond the now, and hearing from God.

Your children's names matter when we call them by what God's word says about them. A good mom doesn't call her children negative names or identify them with things that will damage their minds.

What a mother believes about her children is what often comes to pass. Believe that your children are great assets. Believe that God will make them mighty on the earth. Don't box your children into your limited situation

But let them understand that they have a great purpose, identifying them with the things of God and the word of God. Great moms know that when their children identify with greatness, they will never miss their destiny. Even after death, the names that a mom calls a child will triumph from one generation to the next.

What We Learn from Leah's Example

- Refuse to allow your current adversities to decide the identity of your children.

- Identify your children as God's works of victory in your life.

- Call your children names that reflect God's divine purpose and favor upon them.

- How you refer to your children can be prophetic. Be positive when calling your children so that your words build an identity that can withstand the current negativity.

ELIZABETH

And it came to pass, that on the eighth day they came to circumcise the child; and they called him Zacharias, after the name of his father. And his mother answered and said, not so; but he shall be called John. And they said unto her, There is none of thy kindred that is called this name. And they made signs to his father, how he would have him called. And he asked for a writing table, and wrote, saying, His name is John. And they marvelled all And his mouth was opened immediately, and his tongue loosed, and he spake, and praised God.

Luke 1:59-63

Elizabeth, wife of the priest Zechariah, had to stand and speak a name not common to the people around her. God spoke to her husband while he was in the temple that she would have a son, even though she was barren, and to call his name John. But Zechariah did not believe, and so God took away his speech until the moment he believed.

When the son was born, all the family of Elizabeth and her husband expected a traditional family name. They opposed Elizabeth when she said, his name would be called "John". But her dumb husband spoke after he wrote in confirmation that the child's name would be John, to the amazement of all.

She Spoke God's Word for Her Child in the Face of Doubters

With amazement and awe, God closed the mouths of the unbelievers around Elizabeth when Zechariah confirmed her words, that her son's name was John. Elizabeth knew without a shadow of a doubt that God gave the name to her child. Everyone around her did not believe her when she told them the name.

Like Elizabeth, be bold with the names of your children. Sometimes the enemy tries to use deception as a way for us to accept failure for our children and be comfortable with what others say about them.

Sometimes the enemy will use our friends, surroundings, and also family to minimize the name that God has given our children. Great moms know how to detect these lies and speak up for their children even when the children don't have a voice.

We live in a society where children go through a lot of breakdowns. There are breakdowns in the schools and breakdowns in the home. Amid all the breakdowns children face, moms have to be advocates for them.

Mothers have to be bold as a lion, proclaiming the promises of God's word even when other voices rise to speak against God's word for their children.

Be An Advocate for Your Child's Identity

Many in the world have different opinions about what the identity of our children should be. Often, the public school system in the progressive nations of the West has non-biblical ideas for the identity of our children.

However, even individuals in one's own family can have identity ideas contrary to the teachings of the Bible. Moms have to be advocates for their children when the school system or even relatives are causing our kids to lose sight of their identity and self-esteem.

Great moms will speak what God speaks, no matter what. Keep telling your child that he is called and chosen by God. God has his name in the palm of His hand. Give your child the assurance that God will not leave her or fail her.

When mothers stand for what God said, everything starts to fall into place. Those who want to speak something else on your child will suddenly start to speak what God has spoken. Great moms can put the devil to shame by speaking and praying what God has spoken over their children.

What We Learn from Elizabeth's Example

- Speak God's word over your child even when others around you refuse to believe.

- Speak prophetically and prayerfully over your children.

- Be an advocate for your child's identity in a world that often attacks your child's self-esteem.

3

SECURE AND RECLAIM YOUR CHILDREN

MOSES' MOTHER, JOCHEBED

> And the woman conceived, and bare a son: and
> when she saw him that he was a goodly child,
> she hid him three months. And when she could
> not longer hide him, she took for him an ark
> of bulrushes...and put the child therein; and she
> laid it in the flags by the river's brink.
>
> Exodus 2:2-3

Jochebed was a woman who feared the commandments of God. Although the king of Egypt gave a command for all the male children to be put to death, Jochebed would not give away her child to the system. She decided to fight for and secure her son although everything surrounding him was deadly.

Hide Your Child from the World's Evil

Sometimes, moms have to secure their children by hiding them. Mothers understand that just because the influential voices of the world say something destructive to our children doesn't mean we leave them exposed. Children should be hidden from the hands of the enemy.

In the present time, there are all types of platforms to disengage our children from the things of God. The agenda is to engage children with different types of perversion at an early age.

In the popular music of the culture, the influential entertainers, and the social media influencers, things are being communicated that can damage the spiritual and mental lives of our children. Peer pressure and cultural trends are often pushing our children down the road to spiritual death.

Mothers must be discerning, like Jochebed, and hide their children from the deadly forces. This means making the best effort to keep the dirty songs, videos, and ungodly influencers out of the eyes and ears of our children. Regulate the use of digital devices and fill your home with videos and music that echo the word of God.

Moving May Be Necessary

Jochebed had faith, so she was sure that God had a better plan for her son. When she could no longer hide him, she decided to try something different.

She placed her son in a basket and let him down the Nile River. The Holy Spirit was directing her, even though she did not know what the outcome would be. Pharaoh's daughter saw the child in the river, and she fell in love with Moses.

As a mom, sometimes it will seem like your back is against the wall. You have done all that you can for your child to live, and because of circumstances beyond your control, you have to find a different outlet.

Sometimes that outlet means that you have to leave a certain environment, community, school, and even friendships to secure the child.

Once a Pakistani man got up and moved all his kids out of Seattle, Washington because the hospital system was threatening to change the identity of his children. He brought in his son for depression and suicidal tendencies.

Shortly after, the hospital staff told him that he needed to take his son, now apparently daughter, for gender-affirming care. Learning that the laws of the state could lead to him losing his son to the state system if he did not agree that his son was now a daughter, the Pakistani man agreed to admit his son to a gender-affirming care clinic.

However, instead of going to the clinic, he quit his job and took all his four children to another state that had better parental rights.[1]

The father did what he could to protect his children. He found a different outlet. In the same way, securing your child may mean getting away from places or people who are detrimental to their spiritual and mental health.

Recognize Your Child is a Gift

On the other hand, perhaps your child has grown to the point where you can no longer hide him from the evil influences of the digital world, and other destructive cultural influences.

---

1. Abigail Shrier. City Journal. https://www.city-journal .org/article/when-the-state-comes-for-your-kids, July 8, 2021.

You can still release your child with faith that God will keep him.

Mothers who are insightful, wise, and discerning, like Jochebed, know that their children are a gift from God. Because she saw him as a gift from God, Pharaoh's house also had to come to acknowledge that Moses was special.

Mothers, when you hold on to the gift that God has given you, others will acknowledge your children.

Mothers, remain fearless, and don't throw away your children. Like Jochebed, hide your child and secure their future by not allowing the pressure of others to conquer your vision of your child. The enemy is after our children, so we have to make sure they are covered and secured through prayer and the reading of God's word.

What We Learn from Jochebed's Example

- Securing your children begins with recognizing that they are a gift from God. Your child is a gift that cannot be thrown away but must be protected.

- Hide your child from the evils of the world, the influences of social media, entertainment media, the digital world, and the cultural pressures that can harm your child's spiritual well-being. Do as much as you can to keep them from these ungodly influences.

- To secure your child, it may be necessary to move away from a certain environment or even avoid certain people to protect them from unavoidable evil.

- Believe that God will keep them when it gets to the point that you have to release them into society.

THE MOTHER WHO SCREAMED FOR THE BABY TO LIVE

And this woman's child died in the night; because she overlaid it. And the king said, Divide the living child in two, and give half to the one, and half to the other. Then spake the woman whose the living child was unto the king, for her bowels yearned upon her son, and she said, O my lord, give her the living child...But the other said, Let it be neither mine nor thine, but divide it. Then the king answered...Give her the living child...she is the mother thereof

1 Kings 3:19, 25-27

Two prostitutes with children living in the same house sounds like a recipe for trouble. Well, according to this remarkable story, one woman slept on her baby, and the baby died. The woman with the dead baby replaced the living baby of the other prostitute with her dead baby.

Now it was time for the wise King Solomon to judge the matter. The two women came before the king for him to decide who was the actual mother of the living baby. Wise King Solomon said that the only way to find out is by splitting the living child in two.

The true mother raised her voice and wept for her child to stay alive, even if it meant the other woman keeping him. However, the woman who slept on her child agreed for the child to be cut in two, so neither woman would have him. Solomon immediately knew who the real mother was.

Be Watchful and Know Your Child

When a mother is told her child is about to die, the warrior in her will come alive. The woman with the living child was watchful and knew that the woman who stole her child had rolled over on her baby. When the morning came, she knew that the dead child was not hers. The woman with the living child mourned and wept for her baby.

The woman who rolled over on her child had no remorse, no emotion, and no connection to the living child. Through their carelessness, some have rolled over on the dreams and destiny of their children because they failed to learn what was unique about their child. Now, they are trying to claim your child's gifts and talents for their own gain.

Certain men in the world will try to take advantage of your children's talents for themselves. Learn to reclaim your children from them.

Sometimes the systems of society that we trust, such as the school and entertainment systems, will seek to take ownership of our children, nurturing them for their own goals. After they use up your child, they will present it back to you as if your bad mothering destroyed them. But like the woman of the living child, learn how to reclaim your children.

Cry Out to God

Great moms reclaim their children by being vigilant and watching. They know the uniqueness of their child and can tell when an outside influence is damaging their child's destiny. Give no space to those who want to sabotage the way God commands you to bring up your child.

Cry out to God for the lives of your kids. The God of Justice will hear your cry and not forget your pain. He has never ignored the call of moms crying out for their children. The promise he made from the beginning still stands, the seed of the woman will continue to bruise the head of the devil.

Make Your Voice Heard to Stakeholders

Mothers can make a great difference in their child's future by speaking up for them in society. When my youngest son was in second grade, the teachers decided that he could not learn to read and needed to be placed in a special needs environment. I kept asking for my son to get the necessary tutoring that he needed. When I realized that they were not listening to me, I pulled him out and placed him at another school.

At the new school, my son received the help that he needed and quickly made progress in his reading and academics. Fast forward to today, and my son graduated from high school one year early, after being kept back in second grade.

Make your voice heard by the leading powers and stakeholders in society. Whenever others try to sabotage your Biblical way of raising your children, make your voice heard in the school rooms and city halls of your state.

Do not back down from raising your voice for the physical, spiritual, mental, and emotional well-being of your little ones. Every mother can do her part in letting her voice be heard for the well-being of her children.

What We Learn from the Mother of the Living Child

- Observe your child and know what's unique about him.

- Cry out to God for the well-being of your child.

- On behalf of your child, make your voice heard to the leaders and stakeholders of the society.

SARAH

And Sarah saw the son of Hagar the Egyptian, which she had born unto Abraham, mocking. Wherefore she said unto Abraham, Cast out this bondwoman and her son: for the son of this bondwoman shall not be heir with my son, even with Isaac.

Genesis 21:9-10

God made a promise to Sarah's husband, Abraham, that she would bear a child. But because of her age, she did not believe that the promise would come through her.

In her impatience, she allowed her husband to sleep with her maid so he could have a child. However, God came through with the promise he made Sarah and Abraham and she birthed a child named Isaac, which means "rejoice". Sarah was thankful to the Lord for the miracle that she experienced.

Sarah's son, and the son of her maid both grew. Sadly, Sarah saw that the son of the maid was mocking her son, Isaac. Sarah immediately told her husband to remove the maid, Hagar, and her son, Ishmael, from their home.

Hagar was not a bad person, but the way that Sarah needed to raise her child would cause a problem with the maid. Isaac was the child to receive the promised inheritance, not Ishmael. Conflict was already brewing between the two sons, and only one had the promise of Abraham.

Know God's Promise for Your Children

When someone doesn't believe in your children and they want to cause division in your home, it is your godly right to ask them to leave. Knowing that the hand of God is on your child, interference from others cannot be permitted, or you can lose your way in raising the child. If they don't believe in the promise that God has for your child, the relationship will not work.

Sometimes it's family members who have a problem with raising your child God's way. They want your child to be like them. But God gave you a promise for your child that you cannot compromise.

Separate from those Who Oppose God's Promise for Your Child

At times a friend, neighbor, or family member may mock you for specially raising your child. They may think, "what is so special about your child that they can't do like other children?" They may mock the values you hold for your children and home.

Mothers have to know when to cut off the mockers' access and let them go. They are not there to make your children great. Rather, they are there to belittle and disrespect the call of God upon your children

Mockery is a way to pull mothers down from their purpose. It is a form of pressure for moms to lose confidence in raising their children in God's way. Some will use their connection to you as a mother, to pressure you to raise your kids their way instead of the Bible way.

Great mothers will secure their child's God-given destiny by separating from the people who oppose and influence their child away from God's will.

What We Learn from Sarah

- Know the promise that God has for your children. Ask God to reveal them to you. And, begin with these Biblical promises: Isaiah 54:13, Psalm 112:1-2, Proverbs 20:7, Acts 16:31, Isaiah 49:25.

- Raise your child in God's way so that your children receive the promise God has for them.

- Separate from those who oppose God's promise for your child, and who mock God's way of raising your children.

BIBLICAL PROMISES FOR YOUR CHILDREN

- *Isaiah 54:11 And all thy children shall be taught of the LORD; and great shall be the peace of thy children.*

- *Psalm 112:1-2 Blessed is the man that feareth the LORD, that delighteth greatly in his commandments. His seed shall be mighty upon earth: the generation of the upright shall be blessed.*

- *Proverbs 20:7 The just man walketh in his integrity: his children are blessed after him.*

- *Acts 16:31 ...Believe on the Lord Jesus Christ, and thou shalt be saved, and thy house.*

- *Isaiah 49:25 But thus saith the LORD, Even the captives of the mighty shall be taken away, and the prey of the terrible shall be delivered: for I will contend with him that contendeth with thee, and I will save thy children.*

4

DEDICATE THEIR CHILDREN TO GOD

HANNAH

For this child I prayed; and the LORD hath given me my petition which I asked of him: Therefore also I have lent him to the LORD; as long as he liveth he shall be lent to the LORD. And he worshipped the LORD there.

1 Samuel 1:27-28

Hannah is one of the compelling mothers of the Bible. She was one of two wives of Elkanah. But Hannah was barren while the other woman was bearing children. Barrenness was treated like a curse in those days.

Win at Mothering by Dedicating Your Children

The other wife mocked Hannah for her lack of bearing children. Hannah felt ashamed. Out of the pain of her barrenness, she sought God for a son. She prayed in the temple and made a vow that if God gave her a son, she would give him to the Lord for His service.

Hannah won by dedicating her child to the Lord. While praying in the temple for a child, Eli the priest saw her and thought she was drunk. She was misunderstood as she prayed in her distress.

However, Hannah quickly spoke up and told the priest that she was not drunk but seeking God for a child. When the priest realized that Hannah was indeed praying, he gave her a word of blessing: "*Go in peace: and the God of Israel grant thee thy petition that thou hast asked of him*" (I Samuel 1:17).

Remarkably, Hannah received the blessing and walked in the liberty of the prophetic word the Lord had given her. She was assured that God would grant her request: a son that she would dedicate totally to God's service.

Now she walked into her environment with a new mindset. She had energy again, so she was no longer sad. God was giving her a child that she would raise to be a man of God. She overcame her struggles by dedicating her son to God's work.

You are a mother. And although you are not barren like Hannah, you may at times feel ashamed because you feel unqualified to raise your child. Know that you can overcome your struggles as a mother by dedicating your child to God, like Hannah.

Pray the Prayer of Dedication

When I was younger, I also prayed a prayer like Hannah when I was feeling low. Just before I became a Christian, I was pregnant with my first child outside of marriage. I recall the shameful feeling of becoming a young single mother, but God had a plan for my child.

Living at my mom's house, pregnant, and jobless, I was under a lot of pressure from friends and family members. However, God assured me through the men and women of God in the church.

One night, as I lay on my bed, tears streaming down my face, I cried unto God in prayer and said,

"God, you are the giver of life. You have allowed a child to be inside of me. Lord, I have nothing, but you own everything. I pray that through this child, you will restore my name and take away my shame from my family and those who are talking against me.

"Lord, stop their mouths with your blessing in my life. This child I am bearing in my womb is the work of your hand. God, I have nothing to give this child. I ask you to take this child as your son and do what you wish with the child because you put him in my womb and I am putting him in your hands.

"I give you my broken life and the child, Lord, I give back to you as an offering. Raise him in this world as a man of God. Let him never feel like he is fatherless because you are his father. I dedicate my life and my son to you. We are yours."

My son is now a young man and has traveled to numerous parts of the world, preaching the gospel of Jesus Christ. What if I did not give him to the Lord? Would he be another statistic? I am glad that, like Hannah, the enemy could not completely disable me. Through the power of God, I was able to rebuke the devil and claim the victory.

The Blessings in Dedicating Your Child for Christian Ministry

Hannah's son was Samuel, one of the greatest prophets of Israel. He grew up in the temple and was fully committed to serving God and His people.

God blessed Hannah with many more children because she committed her first son to God's work. Dedicating your child to the Lord and committing him to Christian ministry is an act of victory. God is calling on more mothers today to dedicate their children to his service.

What We Learn from Hannah's Example

- Overcome feelings of inadequacy by dedicating your child to God's service.

- Pray a prayer of dedication to give your son or daughter to God for Christian ministry. Here is a short example: "Lord, I dedicate my life and my child's life to you as an offering. We are yours. Use my child as you please for your glory".

- God will bless mothers who dedicate their children to Christian ministry.

SAMSON'S MOTHER

And the angel of the LORD appeared unto the woman, and said unto her, Behold now, thou art barren, and bearest not: but thou shalt conceive, and bear a son. Now therefore beware, I pray thee, and drink not wine nor strong drink, and eat not any unclean thing: For, lo, thou shalt conceive, and bear a son; and no rasor shall come on his head: for the child shall be a Nazarite unto God from the womb: and he shall begin to deliver Israel out of the hand of the Philistines.

Judges 13:3-5

Even though the Bible never gave her a name, this woman raised an important child. God spoke to the mother of Samson and told her, 'I have seen your barrenness and you will bear a child.'

The angel told the woman that no razor shall touch the child, he shall not have any strong drink, and he shall be a Nazarite. The woman took heed to the message and raised Samson the way that God commanded.

Lead Your Children by God's Word

God had a special purpose for Samson, and his mother played a vital role in his calling. With the rules that came with being a Nazarite, Samson must have seemed different from the other children around him.

However, his mother did not allow their wishes or those of others to dictate how she raised her child. In today's world, some children rebel against their parents and even attempt to boss them. Often the child wants to follow societal trends rather than the values set by parents. But great mothers will hold to Biblical values in raising their children. God told Samson's mother that her child had a specific purpose and a task.

God gave specific instructions for Samson to fulfill his calling. Samson's mother understood that the rise of her son would diminish the camp of their enemy. Therefore, she did her best to follow God's instructions.

Raise Your Child For God's Calling

Good mothers will not neglect the call of God in their children's lives. From an early age, teach your children the word of God. Be an example of living by Biblical teachings in the home and teach your children to do the same.

Hold to holy standards in your household practices. Do not allow the evil devil to corrupt your children from living for God. Keep the standard of holiness in the things you watch, wear, and listen to. Only use positive speech and avoid profanity and harmful insults. Let your home be a place that promotes the teachings of the Bible in word and practice.

Mothers must understand that their children are given for a purpose. In today's society, many women have children and don't understand their purpose. This is why some parents curse and abuse their children.

When the purpose of a child is not understood, it could bring resentment towards the child. However, knowing the child's purpose can bring peace, vision, and understanding of how to raise the child successfully.

Be a Purpose-Driven Parent

Your child may be the one God will use to bring healing to a community or household. There are current problems that are waiting for your child to solve. Your child's birth may be the change that a city or even a nation needs.

God lifted Samson because Israel needed to be freed from their captors. God is often troubled about the state of the world, and he is looking for someone to send to bring a solution. When you follow the commandment of the Lord, you allow God to use your child as a change agent in the world.

Great moms get their children ready for purpose from a young age by gently leading them to Jesus Christ. They use their role to ensure nothing of the devil, unbiblical practices, and values, is in their home.

Further, they will correct their children in love to keep them grounded in Biblical principles. Samson fulfilled his call because his mother was great at following God. Like Samson's mother received the instruction of the angel, open your heart to God's voice to raise your child for God's purpose.

What We Learn from the Example of Samson's Mother

- Raise your children according to the teachings of the Bible.

- Know the call of God on your child and raise them to fulfill that purpose.

- Be a purpose-driven parent so that, from a young age, you are teaching your child, and leading them by example to be a change agent for God.

5

TEACH YOUR CHILDREN THE SCRIPTURES

EUNICE—MOTHER OF TIMOTHY

When I call to remembrance the unfeigned faith
that is in thee, which dwelt first in thy grandmother Lois, and thy mother Eunice; and I am
persuaded that in thee also.

2 Timothy 1:5

E unice was the mother of the biblical character Timothy.
The Apostle Paul, in his letter to Timothy, mentions
the faith of Eunice. The Apostle Paul met Timothy while
on his missionary journey to Lystra. He possibly met Eunice
there. Eunice was a Jewish believer.

Teach Your Kids Bible Scriptures

Paul spoke highly of her faith, saying that she had a sincere one. Her faith was passed down to Timothy. How did Eunice pass down her faith to her son Timothy? We see a clue in 2 Timothy 3:15, where Paul said to Timothy that from a child he knew the scriptures. His mother Eunice was teaching him the Bible from the days of his youth.

Live a True Christian Life

Describing both the faith of Eunice and Timothy's grandmother, Lois, Paul said that it was sincere. We can make some sure conclusions from the sincerity of their faith.

First, they were consistent in applying the word of God to their lives. Secondly, they were women of prayer. Mothers who pray for their children leave a seed on the earth that will not be quenched by the fiery darts of the devil.

Endure Persecution

Moreover, the fact that Eunice was a Jewish believer may have exposed her to persecution or criticism from fellow Jews. Eunice was also married to a Greek, a non-Jew, which could have exasperated the Jews, increasing criticism towards her. Eunice possibly had to endure persecution and doubters of the Christian faith. She kept her faith in Christ even in ill-treatment.

His mother and grandmother's faith were in Timothy's DNA. The gifts that he received from watching his mother kept him safe from skeptics and caused Timothy to stay in the faith. These women's faith left a remarkable example in Timothy. With Timothy as his protege in the ministry, Paul saw the influence of his mother on the life of Timothy.

The way we bring up our children will determine their faith in God. She could have allowed his growth to be on his own, just like so many mothers practice today.

Some mothers allow their children to go to church when they want; they have no fellowship with God. Some young people who grow up in church don't believe that they are going to heaven or even believe in Jesus, yet they are in church every Sunday. They live a separate life from their household.

Eunice understood that if Christianity was going to continue to grow and if the gospel was going to go across the world, she needed to raise her son in the faith. Children need to see our faith and how we handle believing in God in tough times.

Our children need to see that Christianity is not about having physical prosperity but that even through challenges, parents can overcome them through worshiping, praying, and coming together with other believers in Christ.

Timothy grew up in the house seeing his mother cry and pray to God. Timothy saw the passion in her faith since he was there for the hardship. He witnessed her answered prayer; he saw her on her knees, fasting for the believers and caring for the saints. Timothy saw a remarkable example and continued to walk in their footsteps.

What We Learn from the Example of Eunice

- Teach your children Bible scriptures. The Book of Saint John is a good place to start for young children. Have them memorize scriptures such as John 3:16, John 10:10, John 14:6.

- Live an authentic Christian life. Let your child see that whether at church or home, you consistently live for God.

- Endure persecution. Never turn from God no matter how hard it gets.

EARLY MEMORY VERSES FOR YOUNG KIDS

- *John 3:16 For God so loved the world, that he gave his only begotten Son, that whosoever believeth in him should not perish, but have everlasting life.*

- *John 10:10 ...I am come that they might have life, and that they might have it more abundantly.*

- *John 14:6 Jesus saith unto him, I am the way, the truth, and the life: no man cometh unto the Father, but by me.*

KING LEMUEL'S MOTHER

The words of king Lemuel, the prophecy that his mother taught him.

Proverbs 31:1

King Lemuel's mother taught her son the principles of righteousness that make for a successful king. Some Bible scholars have surmised that perhaps King Lemuel is King Solomon. If this is so, then his mother is Bathsheba. She would have been the one to have taught Lemuel how to lead with temperament, wisdom, and knowledge of righteousness.

Whoever King Lemuel was, we know that his mother played an important role in advising him to follow healthy principles as a leader over others. The wisdom she expends on his life led him to be a great judge and a wise king.

Train Your Child to Be a Leader

The king's mother taught him about three vices that can destroy a leader: overindulgence, sexual lust, and pride.

Regarding overindulgence, she taught him that drinking strong drinks would diminish his ability to lead rightfully and would make him lose focus on what is just (Proverbs 31:4-5).

She warned him about giving himself lustfully to women—another destructive vice (Proverbs 31:3). Regarding pride, she told him never to forget the voiceless, poor, and needy (Proverbs 31:8-9).

Guide Your Growing Child on Choosing a Spouse

She also gave guidance to him on how to choose the right woman for a wife. She counseled him to choose a wife that would bring him respect among the people, and to stay away from women that would bring a distraction to the role that God had given him. In summary, she told him that a good woman would fear God, respect him, take care of her home, and work hard.

Teach Your Child Healthy Habits from a Young Age

As a mother, know that your child is destined for greatness. It is your responsibility to teach your child the principles that would allow them to be a positive influence on the earth. Teach your child the scriptures and how they apply in daily living and relating to others.

Self-control, humility, and contentment are three traits to instill into your little ones, so as to guard them against the vices of overindulgence, lust, and pride. Teach them these things as early as possible.

From the infant years, begin to instill in them practices of self-control, humility, and being content with what they have. The mom who teaches leading principles to her children will open doors of greatness for them. It will give them the power to lead and make choices that can bring glory to God.

What We Learn from the Example of King Lemuel's Mother

- Train your child in the principles of great leadership. Start with simply teaching them the commands of scripture and how to apply them to their lives.

- Prepare your children for marriage and guide them in choosing a fitting spouse.

- Instill the habits of self-control, contentment, and humility from a young age to guard them against the king-destroying vices of lust, overindulgence, and pride.

6

FIGHTS FOR THEIR CHILDREN

THE SHUNAMMITE WOMAN

And when she came to the man of God to the
hill, she caught him by the feet: but Gehazi came
near to thrust her away. And the man of God
said, Let her alone; for her soul is vexed within
her: and the LORD hath hid it from me, and
hath not told me. Then she said, Did I desire a
son of my lord? did I not say, Do not deceive me?

2 Kings 4:27-28

The Bible calls the Shunammite woman in this story a
great woman. We see her greatness in how she tended
to the prophet Elisha. She noticed that the man of God had
no place to stay, and convinced her husband to build Elisha a
room to rest as he traveled through their community. For her

kindness, Elisha asked his servant to find out if this insightful woman had any needs.

A Story of Triumph Over Disappointment

The Shunammite woman had a need that she thought would never be fulfilled. It was so hidden within her that only a man of God could discern it. The Shunammite women saw the prophet's need, and the prophet discerned her hidden desire.

She desired to become a mother. However, she resisted the blessing of the prophet because she was afraid of being disappointed. Anyway, through the prophet Elisha, God gave the Shunammite woman her desire for a child. She got pregnant and had a baby. However, a few years later, the child fell sick with a pounding headache, and died. She was now living her worst fear.

She must have felt like her world came crashing down as the child lay there dead. Her faith was being tested, but she remained strong as she believed God for her son. If there was ever a time for her to walk away, that would have been it; but she wrestled with her faith believing that God is faithful. With that in mind, she found the fastest form of transportation she could, and immediately went to find the prophet who gave her the promise of a son. Her husband tried to tell her to wait for another time, but for her the matter was urgent; she needed to see the prophet now.

When she finally reached him Elisha's servant tried to hinder her from reaching the man of God. The man of God perceived that there was a problem and allowed her to see him. Learning of her distress, Elisha went to the child's room, and through prayer, the child came back to life.

While some mothers would bury their children and question their faith in God, the Shunammite kept her testimony. She chased after the man of God to save her child. Do not bury your promise because things look down. Don't move on from your children when difficult problems come into their lives. Fight for the well-being of your children.

Get Help When Needed

In hard times, great moms must seek help for the success of their children. Mothers will chase, plead, and fight for their children. Death, drugs, depression, gangs, crime, and more have taken the lives of so many young people. These are young people with promise and vision, but they are stunted by death or evil works.

They are either physically taken or spiritually hindered. If not death, the devil plans to limit your child's state of mind so that they never reach their full potential. When you have done all that you can, reach out to other Christians who can pray. Bring your child to a pastor or leader who can help to deliver your child from the things that bind him.

Don't Give Up On Your Child

In reality, there is nothing wrong with crying. When mothers fight for their children with tears and mourning, God will hear from heaven and deliver the child. God will bend the heavens and come down to fight for the seed.

Don't give up when there are obstacles for your child to break through in life. Don't give up on a child who has left home or is on drugs. Don't give up on a child who has backslidden from the faith.

God will hear if you continue to pursue. Believe that your child was given by God to make a difference in the world. When you cry, God will crush the devil's head so your child can fulfill his purpose.

Get the Support of Your Church

It is important to have someone of faith to help you fight for your child. Find a real church that believes in the power of the Holy Spirit. A church that teaches the word of God.

A church under God's agenda, not an entertainment-driven church. A church that seeks God's face and hears from Him.

Elisha brought the child back to life, but One greater than Elisha is now with us. Jesus is here; the tabernacle of God is with us. We just need to believe in his power and fight. Fight by laying hands on your child and rebuke evil spirits from their lives. Fight by praying for your children daily. Fight by speaking the promises of God over their lives. Most parents would have buried the child and moved on with life. But we learn from the Shunammite woman how to fight by faith.

What We Learn from the Example of the Shunammite

- Keep your faith alive when disappointing things occur in the lives of your children.

- Seek the help of a spiritual leader such as your pastor and get the support of your church community.

- Don't give up on your child. Continue praying and believing.

- Fight by faith by laying hands and praying over your children. Speak the promises of God's word over their life. Here are some scripture promises to start with: Isaiah 54:13, Psalm 112:1-2, Proverbs 20:7, Acts 16:31.

THE CANAANITE WOMAN

Then came she and worshipped him, saying, Lord, help me. But he answered and said, It is not meet to take the children's bread, and to cast it to dogs. **27.** And she said, Truth, Lord: yet the dogs eat of the crumbs which fall from their masters' table. **28.** Then Jesus answered and said unto her, O woman, great is thy faith: be it unto thee even as thou wilt. And her daughter was made whole from that very hour.

Matthew 15:25-28

Like the Shunammite, she was not a Jew, but she held to the promises of God by faith. The Canaanite woman was outside the commonwealth of Israel, but she had a need. Her daughter was being tormented by a demonic spirit. But she heard of Jesus.

When she came and asked Him to free her daughter, Jesus said basically, "I can't because you are a dog."

How many would have walked away from Jesus because his statement seemed out of touch with his reputation?

Your Faith Will Be Tested

However, nothing could have been further from the truth. Jesus came for the lost soul, but there are times when God tests our faith. It seems like Jesus was insulting the Canaanite woman. But she understood how faith in God works, and her faith was being tested by Jesus himself.

The Canaanite woman was an outsider, and his disciples noticed that she was being a nuisance to Christ. They ordered her to be sent away and Jesus said not a word. For a little while, he allowed her to be humiliated and feel ashamed.

Don't Give Up When Your Prayers Have Not Been Answered

When God doesn't answer your prayers for your child right away, it does not mean all hope is lost. If a child is acting out at home and you may be praying but not receiving an answer, keep speaking the word of God until you see the change in your child. A demonic spirit may be trying to destroy your child, but by faith in God, your child will be free.

God will come through for you at the level of your faith. As a godly mother, God will allow your faith to be tested because he already knows where you stand. He already identifies the level of faith that you stand on, and therefore, he can put you through a test.

For a moment, you may feel humiliated. Your child seems to be under the devil's influence even though you did your best to raise him in God. God knows you can handle the humiliation because of your lifestyle of faith.

Speak by Faith Even in the Lowest Moments

Jesus knew that the child would be made free. The Canaanite's willingness to accept the moniker that she was a dog, and yet extend her faith to receive was a powerful display of sincere faith. Our faith conviction even when things look bad and others look down on us, will bring deliverance to the life of our children. Your child will be made whole.

What We Learn from the Example of the Canaanite

- There are times when the faith you have for the well-being of your children will be tested.

- Continue praying for your children, even when you don't immediately receive the answer.

- Speak by faith, even when the circumstances in your child's life leave you feeling humiliated.

7

SUPPORT YOUR CHILDREN TO REACH THEIR DESTINY

REBEKAH

And the children struggled together within her; and she said, If it be so, why am I thus? And she went to inquire of the LORD. And the LORD said unto her, Two nations are in thy womb...and the elder shall serve the younger.

Genesis 25:22-23

R ealizing something was unusual about her pregnancy, Rebekah asked God about it. He prophetically spoke to her concerning her children.

Ask God About Your Children

God told her she was pregnant with twins, and that both her children would lead a great nation, but the younger would be greater. Rebekah understood and trusted God's plan and she never backed down in making sure it was accomplished.

The mark of God was on her sons, but God had a certain order in which he wanted to execute the call. The younger son would inherit the promise of the firstborn. Rebekah understood and played a supporting role in ensuring the plan was accomplished. She guided her younger son Jacob to secure the promise and to inherit the birthright given through prophecy.

The Bible tells us that Rebekah was close to her younger son Jacob. But Isaac, the father, seemed to be fond of his older son Esau because he was a hunter. When it was time for Isaac to pass the blessings of the firstborn son to Esau, Rebekah helped the younger son Jacob to dress like his older brother and go to his father, who was blind, to receive the firstborn blessings.

Do Your Best to Support Your Child's Calling

So, it seems Rebekah supported her son by tricking her husband, Isaac. Also, some would say Rebekah was showing favoritism. Even though this may be true, the key is to understand that it was God's will for Jacob, the younger, to inherit the firstborn blessing. Rebekah knew this from the revelation God gave her when she was pregnant. And even though Rebekah did not go through with it the best way, God used her frailty to fulfill His will. Was Rebekah showing favoritism or just recognizing the differing callings on her children?

Her action is a testimony of her unwavering commitment to making sure that what God told her came to pass. She passed down a legacy of faith in how a mother should support God's word on her child.

Support Each Child's Unique Gifts

I am not advocating using trickery or showing favoritism. Only that as mothers, we need to have insight concerning our children. Each of your children has unique gifts and a calling from God. Through prayer, we can understand God's general plan for our children, and build a support system for each of them to succeed.

Our job is not to question what God has rendered in our children's lives, but to simply be a help and support for it to happen. One of them may become the next mayor of a city, the other an entrepreneur, and the next a pastor. In the end, Esau became the father of a great nation, and Jacob the father of Israel, God's chosen people.

If God gives you a word concerning your children, be the number one supporter of what God said. Write it on the walls, speak it over them, pray it in the open. Run with it and be watchful so that God can give the victory in due time.

Do your best. Don't use trickery. But if you have true faith, even in your frailty, God will bring to pass what he says about your child.

What We Learn from the Example of Rebekah

- Seek God in prayer to know what His purpose is for each of your children.

- To the best of your ability, support your child's unique gift and calling.

BATHSHEBA

And of all my sons—for the LORD has given me many sons—he has chosen my son Solomon to sit on the throne of the LORD's kingship over Israel. For he said to me: It is your son Solomon who shall build my house and my courts, for I have chosen him for my son, and I will be a father to him.

1 Chronicles 28:5-6

Bathsheba, King Solomon's mother, was taken by king David from Uriah, her previous husband. David committed adultery with her.

Bathsheba became pregnant, and to cover the infidelity, David had her husband killed in battle. The Lord was not pleased with David's sin. A consequence of the sin was that Bathsheba and David's first child died. However, Bathsheba became pregnant again, and the second child was Solomon.

Overcome Past Mistakes by Being a Great Mother Today

Since David was king, it was difficult for Bathsheba to resist David's decision to have an adulterous affair with her. She came to know the pain of losing her child and her husband because of David's sin. But within her was the strength to carry on. God gave her a second chance and more children.

Through her loss, Bathsheba learned a valuable lesson: She would have to teach her son the value of wisdom and understanding. Bathsheba became an advocate for her son's right to the throne inside the kingdom, and through her, David remembered Solomon.

Through the prophecy of the prophet Nathan, David knew from God that Solomon would build his temple and succeed him as king of Israel. However, as David got weaker because of old age, another of his sons, Adonijah, rose and declared himself king.

The prophet Nathan came and told Bathsheba that Adonijah was trying to take the kingdom from her son. We can assume that since Nathan gave the original prophecy, he knew that the rightful heir to the throne was Solomon.

Advocate for Your Child's Future

The prophet Nathan counseled Bathsheba to go see the king. She immediately went and stood before the king, telling him all that Adonijah had done. Bathsheba knew that if she did not go before the king, the lives of those who stood with David would be lost, including hers and Solomon's.

While she was telling the king of the plot, Nathan the prophet came in after and confirmed the words of Bathsheba. As she stood in his presence, he made an oath before her and assured her that Solomon, her son, would be king.

The willingness of the prophet Nathan to counsel and support Bathsheba to ensure Solomon was the next king is a testament to her motherhood. The prophet came to her to reveal Adonijah's plan. Bathsheba's quick action defeated the plot of Adonijah, and she got the confirmation that was needed for David to move on behalf of Solomon.

Nurture Your Child to Greatness

As mothers, we go through pain and some things happen in our lives that we don't want to be reminded of, whether a broken relationship or the loss of a child.

Just like the mothers of today, Bathsheba went through shame, disappointment, pain, and loss. Though she lost her first child, she nurtured the second one into becoming the king of Israel.

Nurture the gift that is within your children. Teach them in wisdom, and show them the way of God, even when things seem hard. Stay in church even when things seem hard. Don't allow your children to be raised by worldly associations.

Bathsheba spoke on her son's behalf because she was associated with the prophet and the priest. They stood by what David said because of her good report on raising her son.

The world may see your faults and know your weaknesses, but raise your children to grow in wisdom and understanding. While you may have failed in the past, you have victory today in raising your child for God's purpose.

Don't allow people who don't have wisdom and understanding to be among your children. Learn to weed out the things that would want to take away the royal position God has given your child. Bathsheba raised one of the greatest kings on the earth. There was none as wise as Solomon. When God's Hand is upon your child, you have to protect and support your child.

What We Learn from Bathsheba's Example

- Despite your past mistakes, you can be a great mother today.

- Build a positive relationship with your husband, and with men and women of God who can speak into the life of your children. Bathsheba clearly had a good relationship with her husband and the prophet Nathan.

- Be an advocate for your child. Boldly speak up to ensure that they receive the great things that are set for them.

8

THE FINAL VISION OF A GREAT MOTHER

And there appeared a great wonder in heaven;
a woman clothed with the sun, and the moon
under her feet, and upon her head a crown of
twelve stars: And she being with child cried,
travailing in birth, and pained to be delivered.

Revelations 12:1-2

The apostle John had a mysterious vision of a mother, a woman clothed with the sun, the moon as her shoes, and twelve stars as her crown. The vision gives us a summary of the spiritual battle every mother faces.

Bible scholars have differing opinions on who she represents. Some scholars believe that she was the Church, and others believe that she is Israel. She is probably a symbol of both

Israel and the Church. Either way, she was a mother running to save her child.

This woman was pregnant. The dragon, the old serpent, the devil, watched her, ready to devour her child as soon as she delivered. Similarly, the devil hates mothers and their offspring, and is waiting to destroy them.

She delivered a male child who would rule all nations. The child was caught up to God, and His Throne. This child is Jesus Christ. Even though the devil tried to kill him, Jesus Christ was victorious and today is at the right hand of God. Be assured, mothers, that God will give your children victory if you put your trust in Him. Though the devil will try to harm them, God will give them a way out.

Now that the child was safe, how about the mother? God had prepared a place for her in the wilderness where she remained safe for a while. Mom, God knows how to keep you safe.

Soon after, the dragon's anger increased against the woman because he was losing his war against the kingdom of God. Brought down to earth, the old serpent went after the mother to persecute her. But God gave her the wings of an eagle to fly away to safety. Mom, the devil won't give up trying to harm you because he is angry that you gave birth to a child of purpose. But don't worry. God will give you eagle wings to fly away and rest from the attacks of the devil.

The serpent proceeded to cast water out of his mouth to flood her out of the place God had for her. But then the earth opened her mouth and swallowed up the flood that came against her.

Again, God's protective hand remains over mothers. When the dragon realized that the woman was protected, he went after her remaining children, those who keep the testimony of Jesus Christ.

As a mother, once your seed is on the earth, there will be a war against you. Whether it is emotional, mental, or physical, the devil will stop at nothing to see you suffer because he knows every child that is born on the earth is a potential danger to his kingdom. As Christian mothers, we are more prone to the attack of the devil because he knows that we are raising children for the kingdom of God. In the same way, the dragon went after the seed of the woman, he will also seek to go after any godly seed on the earth.

Throughout the Bible, we have seen weak mothers fight through their children. We have seen her win wars with her wisdom. We have seen her defeat nations with her tears.

Her birth pain is always remembered in the sight of God. No matter what the world says about her children, she will always persevere and prove them wrong.

Like with the mysterious mother of Revelation 12, as you raise your children unto the Lord, he will send you help. God will give you revelation concerning your children.

God will allow you to be hidden from those who seek to demonize, belittle, or destroy you and your seed. God will dispatch the angels of heaven to war on your behalf. He will order the earth to make room for you. God will give you and your children an abundance of life.

BE LIKE MARY, THE WILLING VESSEL

And Mary said, Behold the handmaid of the Lord; be it unto me according to thy word...sacrifice to

Luke 1:38

A sure thing about the woman of Revelation is that she willingly became a vessel for the man-child that ascended. While the symbol of the woman extends beyond one person, we surely see a symbolic reference to Mary, the mother of Jesus.

The characteristic of Mary that made a huge difference was her willingness to be a vessel for Christ to enter the earth. She was a virgin. Her pregnancy would cause questions, and possibly accusations of infidelity. Joseph, her fiancé, even thought of ending the relationship. Even with all the potential questions the pregnancy would cause, Mary was willing to be the womb through which the Messiah would be born. She was a willing vessel to be a womb for the savior. Are you willing to let your life be a womb through which God can accomplish his purpose in the next generation? Are you willing to sacrifice to raise a child who will bring glory to God? God simply asks for a willing vessel who he can use as a womb for His purpose. To sum up the lives of the great mothers of the Bible—they were willing vessels for God's purpose.

REFLECTION

After reading through the book, identify three actions that you can immediately apply to influence your child to fulfill God's purpose.

> ....
>
>
>
>
>
> ....

Name two specific ways you can build your child's identity in Christ (Refer to Chapter 2 for inspiration).

> ....
>
>
>
>
>
> ....

Prayerfully identify the unique gifts that your child may have from God. Does your child have a passion for ministry or a good cause?

Has the Lord spoken to you about your child's destiny and purpose? If not, talk to God like Rebekah did, and ask him about the future of your child. God speaks to mothers about their children. Listen to Him.

OTHER BOOKS FROM

HARVESTERS ONLINE

We publish and produce books, blogs, podcasts, pamphlets, videos, training courses, and other digital content to equip Christian believers to be instruments for world revival.

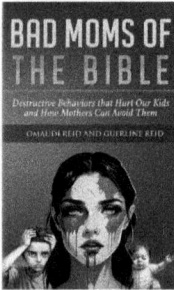

If you learned from "**Great Moms of the Bible**", you will also enjoy "*Bad Moms of the Bible: Destructive Behavior That Hurts Our Kids And How Mothers Can Avoid Them*". "*Bad Moms of the Bible*" looks at the negative example of 7 notorious moms of the Bible. Learn about the behaviors that can harm your children spiritually, emotionally, and physically, and how to avoid them.

ABOUT THE AUTHOR

Apostle G. Reid, is a powerful preacher, representing Christ in different parts of the earth. She has been married for over 25 years to Bishop O. Reid. And, she is the mother of three children.

www.ingramcontent.com/pod-product-compliance
Lightning Source LLC
Chambersburg PA
CBHW072148090426
42739CB00013B/3313